BIBLE INFOGRAPHICS

FOR KIDS™ EPIC GUIDE TO JESUS

HARVEST kids

HARVEST HOUSE PUBLISHERS
EUGENE, OREGON

CREATED BY

HARVEST HOUSE
BIBLE
INFOGRAPHICS
TEAM

Illustrations by
BRIAN HURST

HEATHER GREEN   **AARON DILLON**   **KYLE HATFIELD**   **NICOLE DOUGHERTY**   **KYLER DOUGHERTY**

SPECIAL THANKS →   AMBER HOLCOMB   KEN CARSON   GENE SKINNER

All Bible Infographics for Kids™ family of products, including *Bible Infographics for Kids™ Epic Guide to Jesus*, are recipients of the prestigious and world-renowned **SEAL OF APPROVAL** as well as the much respected and selectively awarded **AWESOME CERTIFICATION.**

Seals of Approval and Awesome Certifications are granted by the Bible Infographics Development Team to the highest quality and most craze-mazing Bible Infographic material and content produced by the Bible Infographics Development Team. *It's very serious, and not just marketing hype.* 😊

Disclaimer: THESE AWARDS DO NOT PROVIDE ACTUAL MERIT IN ANY CAPACITY
The awards and certifications listed above, including but not limited to, graphics, text, and other material written are for hilarious purposes only. No awards on this page are intended to be substitutes for actual professional awards, certifications, or merit-based acknowledgments. Always seek the advice of legitimate award-giving professionals or qualified certification officiants with any questions you may have regarding being certified awesome or attaining a seal of approval. Never undertake the care of actual seals, self-designate seals of approval, or bestow awesomeness certifications without the consultation of craze-mazing professionals.

Bible Infographics for Kids™ Epic Guide to Jesus
Copyright © 2022 by Harvest House Publishers
Published by Harvest House Publishers
Eugene, Oregon 97408
www.harvesthousepublishers.com

ISBN 978-0-7369-8421-8 (hardcover)
Library of Congress Control Number: 2017028151

Printed in China
21 22 23 24 25 26 27 28 29 30 / RDS / 10 9 8 7 6 5 4 3 2 1

Bible Infographics for Kids™ Epic Guide to Jesus

is your incredible infographic invitation that immerses you in the **life**, **times**, and **ministry** of Jesus.

...and the quiz is on Monday. Any questions?

WAIT, WHAT IS AN INFOGRAPHIC?

Well, first you should know if you've bought and read the other Bible Infographics for Kids™ books. But since you asked, just know that infographics help you see information using a combination of fun facts and craze-mazing visuals.

INFOGRAPHICS 101
Intro to Infographics

And fair warning! Reading this book may cause side effects* like—

Required reassembly of one's blown mind

Complete captivation with Jesus's culture

Extra excitement examining the evidence of Jesus's life

Full-blown faith in His mind-blowing miracles and triumphant teachings

Incomparable insight into His death and resurrection

DISCOVER JESUS IN THE ENTIRE BIBLE

as you learn about His culture, those who loved Him and those who opposed Him, the amazing events connected to Him, and so much more.

__No harmful side effects have been found after reading this book,__ even after the recommended multiple times. Results from reading this book may include minor papercuts and a deeper understanding of Jesus.

CONTENTS

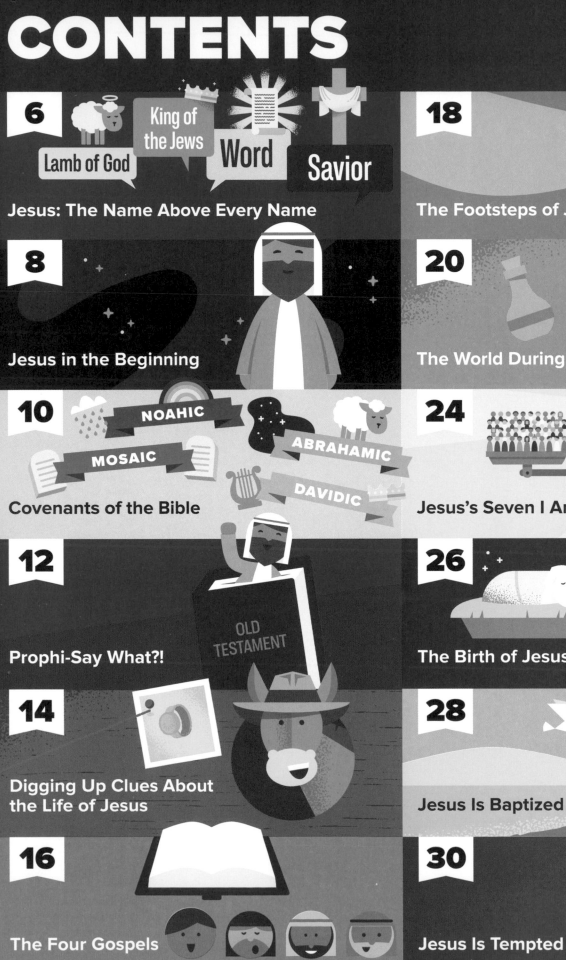

JESUS : THE NAME ABOVE EVERY NAME

(and all the other names of Jesus)

Hebrew	Meaning
α Greek	Key verse

Jesus

Paul

ℵ יְשׁוּעָה • yeshua
α Ἰησοῦς • iēsous
🔍 Jehovah is salvation
🔖 Philippians 2:9-11

DID YOU KNOW that the man who was released instead of Jesus was also named Jesus? Jesus Barabbas. But many versions of the Bible just include the name Barabbas.

Christ / Messiah / Anointed One

Andrew

α Χριστός • christos
α Μεσσίας • messias
🔍 anointed one or messiah
🔖 John 1:41

Lamb of God
John the Baptist

α ἀμνός • amnos   🔍 Lamb
α θεός • theos   🔍 God
🔖 John 1:29,36

Immanuel
Isaiah

ℵ עִמָּנוּאֵל • ʿImmanuw'el   🔍 Lamb
α Ἐμμανουήλ • emmanouēl   🔍 God
🔍 God with us
🔖 Isaiah 7:14

Son of God
Martha

α υἱός • yhios   🔍 Son
α θεός • theos   🔍 God
🔖 John 11:27

Son of Man
Jesus

α υἱός • yhios   🔍 Son
α ἄνθρωπος • anthrōpos 🔍 Man
🔖 Mark 10:45

Son of David
Matthew

α υἱός • yhios   🔍 Son
α Δαβίδ • dabid   🔍 David
🔖 Matthew 1:1

The people who testified to Jesus being the Son of God include God the Father, the angel Gabriel, apostles Peter and Paul, demons, and Jesus Himself.

Why would Jesus call Himself the Son of Man? Maybe to remind people of His humanity, or maybe He was referring to a messianic prophecy in Daniel 7:13-14.

NUMBER OF TIMES EACH NAME OF JESUS IS USED IN THE BIBLE*

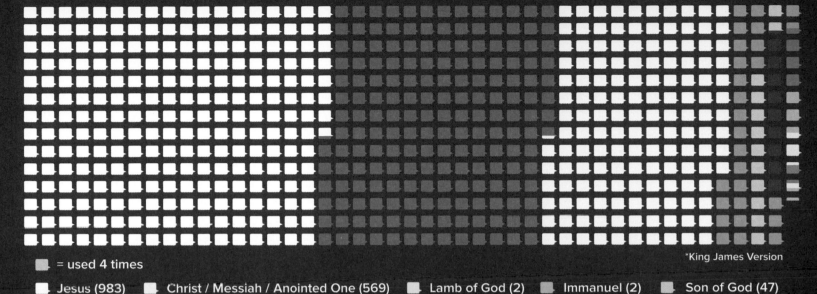

*King James Version

■ = used 4 times

■ Jesus (983)   ■ Christ / Messiah / Anointed One (569)   ■ Lamb of God (2)   ■ Immanuel (2)   ■ Son of God (47)

■ Son of Man (88)   ■ Son of David (14)   ■ King of the Jews (18)   ■ Lord / Master (732)   ■ Saviour (37)

■ Word (7)   ■ Rabbi / Rabboni (10)   ■ Alpha and Omega (4)

King of the Jews

The Magi

α βασιλεύς • basileus   🔍 King
α Ἰουδαῖος • ioudaios   🔍 Jews
🔖 Matthew 2:1-2

Lord/Master

The Disciples

α κύριος • kyrios
🔍 Sovereign, master, owner
🔖 Luke 8:24

Savior

α σωτήρ • so-ta'r
🔍 deliverer
🔖 Luke 2:11

Word

John

α λόγος • logos
🔍 In the gospel of John, refers to Jesus Christ
🔖 John 3:1-2

Rabbi

Mary Magdalene

α ῥαββί • rhabbi
🔍 Teacher
🔖 John 20:16

❗ Judas called Jesus "Rabbi" when he betrayed Him.

Alpha & Omega

α ἄλφα • alpha   🔍 first letter in the Greek alphabet
α Ω • omega   🔍 last letter in the Greek alphabet
🔍 Christ is the beginning and the end.
🔖 Revelation 22:13

Did you know the world record for the longest name is 747 characters long?

JESUS IN THE

JESUS IN ETERNITY

Jesus existed before the heavens and the earth were created. (Colossians 1:17)
Three of His titles remind us of His eternal nature:

I AM • John 8:56-59

When Jesus said,
"Before Abraham was born, I am,"
He wasn't using poor grammar!
He was saying that He has always existed without beginning or end.
(Mind-blowing, we know.)

He was also referencing Exodus 3:14-15, where God says to Moses,
"I am who I am."

Jesus was claiming to be the same God who led Israel out of Egypt centuries earlier.

the Word • John 1:1

This doesn't mean Jesus is a literal word composed of letters and sounds.

In Greek, this is the term **"logos."**

Logos reveals the truth, substance, and reasoning behind the words.

Part of Jesus's purpose is to reveal the truth of God to us.

the Son • John 17:1,5

The three persons of God **lived for eternity past together.**

The Father | The Son | The Spirit

Jesus's role as the Son was to carry out the Father's plan.

JESUS IN CREATION

WHAT did He create?

Everything!
Colossians 1:16

In fact, there was **nothing made that wasn't made by Jesus.**
John 1:3

HOW did He create?

God created everything through **the Word** (which was Jesus), speaking everything into existence.

WHY did He create?

God the Father, the Son, and the Holy Spirit wanted to **share Their love**, so They created the universe.

BEGINNING

JESUS IN THE OLD TESTAMENT

Jesus shows up several times in the Bible before being born as a human.

theophanies (n.): appearances of God in human form

God the Father cannot be seen in physical form, so when people saw God in the Old Testament, they were actually seeing Jesus (John 1:18).

Many of these times Jesus is called the "angel [messenger] of the Lord."

HAGAR
Genesis 16:7-12

When Sarah sent her servant Hagar away, the angel of the Lord found her by a spring of water and announced to her that she would have a son named Ishmael.

ABRAHAM
Genesis 18:1 20

The Lord appeared to Abraham to promise that he and Sarah would have a son within a year, and to announce His intent to destroy Sodom.

MOSES
Exodus 3:1-5

The angel of the Lord appeared to Moses from a burning bush and told him that He would deliver Israel from slavery in Egypt.

JOSHUA
Joshua 5:13-15

The commander of the Lord's army appeared to Joshua and told him how Israel would conquer the city of Jericho.

GIDEON
Exodus 3:1-5

The angel of the Lord appeared to Gideon and told him that He would be with him as he led his army against the Midianites.

ISAIAH
Isaiah 6:1-4

Isaiah had a vision of the Lord seated on a throne in heaven. The apostle John says that Isaiah saw Jesus's glory (John 12:41).

COVENANTS OF THE BIBLE

IN THE OLD TESTAMENT, GOD MADE SEVERAL COVENANTS WITH HIS PEOPLE.

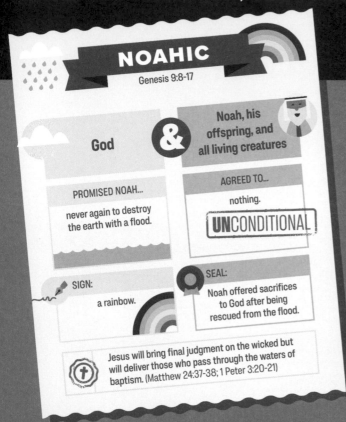

NOAHIC
Genesis 9:8-17

God & **Noah, his offspring, and all living creatures**

PROMISED NOAH...
never again to destroy the earth with a flood.

AGREED TO...
nothing.
UNCONDITIONAL

SIGN:
a rainbow.

SEAL:
Noah offered sacrifices to God after being rescued from the flood.

Jesus will bring final judgment on the wicked but will deliver those who pass through the waters of baptism. (Matthew 24:37-38; 1 Peter 3:20-21)

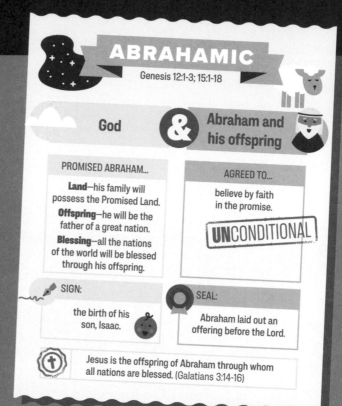

ABRAHAMIC
Genesis 12:1-3; 15:1-18

God & **Abraham and his offspring**

PROMISED ABRAHAM...
Land—his family will possess the Promised Land.
Offspring—he will be the father of a great nation.
Blessing—all the nations of the world will be blessed through his offspring.

AGREED TO...
believe by faith in the promise.
UNCONDITIONAL

SIGN:
the birth of his son, Isaac.

SEAL:
Abraham laid out an offering before the Lord.

Jesus is the offspring of Abraham through whom all nations are blessed. (Galatians 3:14-16)

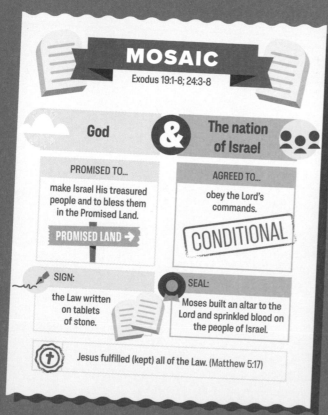

MOSAIC
Exodus 19:1-8; 24:3-8

God & **The nation of Israel**

PROMISED TO...
make Israel His treasured people and to bless them in the Promised Land.
PROMISED LAND →

AGREED TO...
obey the Lord's commands.
CONDITIONAL

SIGN:
the Law written on tablets of stone.

SEAL:
Moses built an altar to the Lord and sprinkled blood on the people of Israel.

Jesus fulfilled (kept) all of the Law. (Matthew 5:17)

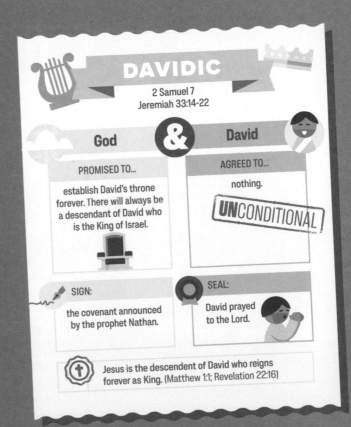

DAVIDIC
2 Samuel 7
Jeremiah 33:14-22

God & **David**

PROMISED TO...
establish David's throne forever. There will always be a descendant of David who is the King of Israel.

AGREED TO...
nothing.
UNCONDITIONAL

SIGN:
the covenant announced by the prophet Nathan.

SEAL:
David prayed to the Lord.

Jesus is the descendent of David who reigns forever as King. (Matthew 1:1; Revelation 22:16)

A COVENANT is an agreement between two or more people. It is more than just a contract—it is the foundation of a relationship (like a marriage).

A CONTRACT is an agreement between people about a transaction (like buying a car).

God made two types of covenants with His people:

 CONDITIONAL

UNCONDITIONAL

Conditional covenants:
The people **agree to** obey God, and God **promises to** bless the people.

Unconditional covenants:
God **promises to** bless the people **regardless** of what the people do.

All covenants were made with...

A SIGN
a visible expression that God has **agreed to** the covenant, much like a signature on a contract.

A SEAL
an activity or expression that the person understands the terms of the covenant and **agrees to** them.

Nope, not that kind of seal!

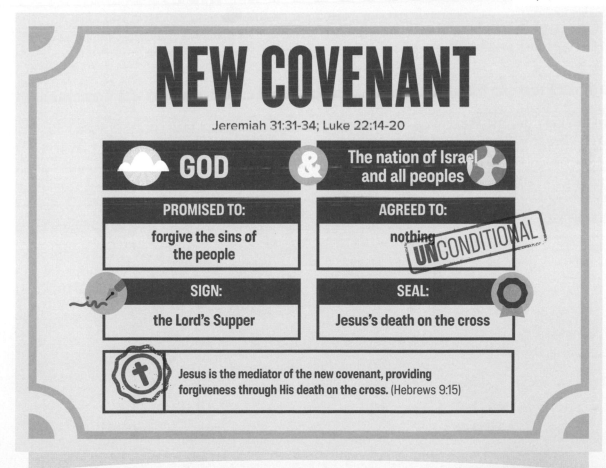

NEW COVENANT

Jeremiah 31:31-34; Luke 22:14-20

☁ GOD	&	🌍 The nation of Israel and all peoples

PROMISED TO:	AGREED TO:
forgive the sins of the people	nothing *UNCONDITIONAL*

SIGN:	SEAL:
the Lord's Supper	Jesus's death on the cross

✝ Jesus is the mediator of the new covenant, providing forgiveness through His death on the cross. (Hebrews 9:15)

All the covenants in the Old Testament are fulfilled in Jesus.

He is the one who fulfills all of God's promises in the covenants. (2 Corinthians 1:20)

PROPHI-SAY WHAT?!

JESUS WAS IN THE OLD TESTAMENT TOO!

It's amazing to think that hundreds of years before Jesus was born, people knew He was coming! Messianic prophecies were written throughout the Old Testament to tell us about Christ and all the amazing things He'd do!

For example, check out Zechariah 9:9!

Spoiler alert: It was God.

Who could have written something so detailed and accurate?

THE BOOKS OF THE BIBLE COMBINE TO GIVE US AN AMAZING, COHESIVE STORY.

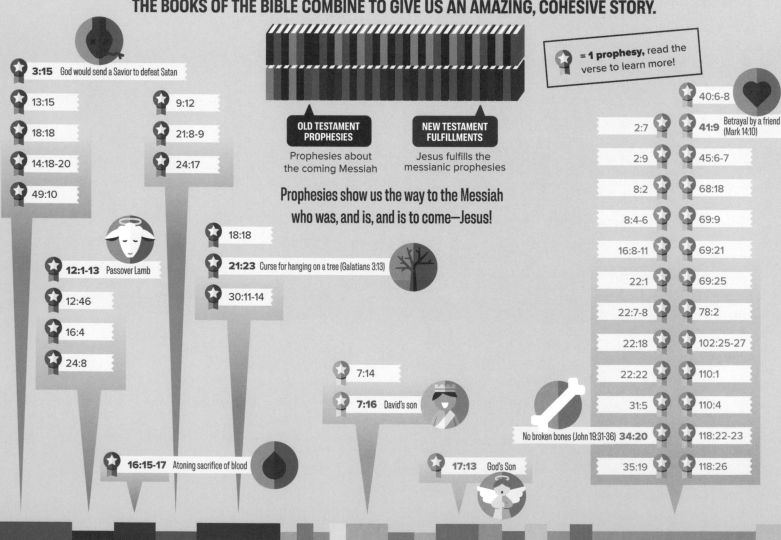

3:15 God would send a Savior to defeat Satan

13:15

18:18

14:18-20

49:10

9:12

21:8-9

24:17

OLD TESTAMENT PROPHESIES
Prophesies about the coming Messiah

NEW TESTAMENT FULFILLMENTS
Jesus fulfills the messianic prophesies

Prophesies show us the way to the Messiah who was, and is, and is to come—Jesus!

⭐ = **1 prophesy**, read the verse to learn more!

40:6-8

2:7 · **41:9** Betrayal by a friend (Mark 14:10)

2:9 · **45:6-7**

8:2 · **68:18**

8:4-6 · **69:9**

16:8-11 · **69:21**

22:1 · **69:25**

22:7-8 · **78:2**

22:18 · **102:25-27**

22:22 · **110:1**

31:5 · **110:4**

No broken bones (John 19:31-36) **34:20** · **118:22-23**

35:19 · **118:26**

12:1-13 Passover Lamb

12:46

16:4

24:8

18:18

21:23 Curse for hanging on a tree (Galatians 3:13)

30:11-14

7:14

7:16 David's son

16:15-17 Atoning sacrifice of blood

17:13 God's Son

GENESIS EXODUS LEVITICUS NUMBERS DEUTERONOMY JOSHUA JUDGES RUTH 1ST SAMUEL 2ND SAMUEL 1ST KINGS 2ND KINGS 1ST CHRONICLES 2ND CHRONICLES EZRA NEHEMIAH ESTHER JOB PSALMS PROVERBS

"He said to them, 'This is what I told you while I was still with you: Everything must be fulfilled that is written about me in **THE LAW OF MOSES,** **THE PROPHETS** and **THE PSALMS** .' "

Luke 24:44

! The books of the Hebrew Bible (the Old Testament) were divided by genre. Each genre had a different use in Jewish worship and was read in different ways.

! Prophecies show us that we can have full confidence that God delivers on His promises!

Virgin birth (Matthew 1:18)   6:9-10   49:6   **POW!**

7:14   **50:6**   Beating and spitting (Mark 14:65)

8:14   53:1-5

9:1-2   **53:7-8**   Suffering Lamb of God (Mark 15:4-5)

9:6-7   **53:9**   Sinless servant of God (1 Peter 2:22)

11:2   **53:9**   Buried in a rich man's grave (Matthew 27:57-60)

11:10   53:12

22:22   55:3

The Spirit of the Lord, Wisdom (Luke 2:52)   **35:5-6**   59:20-21

40:3-5   60:1-3

42:1-4   65:1

Blindness and deafness healed (Matthew 11:5)   45:23   65:2

7:13-14

7:27

9:24-26

23:5-6

31:15

31:31-34   New Covenant

37:24-26

11:1   Jesus to return from Egypt

1:17

9:11-12

3:1

The spirit of Elijah would precede the Messiah   **4:5-6**

5:2   Ruler born in Bethlehem (Matthew 2:1)

5:2   Eternal ruler (Matthew 2:1)

5:4-5

Thirty pieces of silver (Matthew 27:1-10)   **11:12-13**   9:9

12:10

13:7

ECCLESIASTES   SONG OF SOLOMON   ISAIAH   JEREMIAH   LAMENTATIONS   EZEKIEL   DANIEL   HOSEA   JOEL   AMOS   OBADIAH   JONAH   MICAH   NAHUM   HABAKKUK   ZEPHANIAH   HAGGAI   ZECHARIAH   MALACHI

Digging Up Clues About the
LIFE of JESUS

To get more clues about Jesus and His life, we can look at other **historical texts** (in addition to the Bible) and see **archaeological evidence** from Jesus's lifetime.

historical text

archaeological evidence

 Author   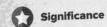 **Year found**

★ **Significance**   📖 **In the Bible**

The True Word

👤 written by Celsus, a Greek philosopher (AD 176)

★ Mentions both Christianity and Judaism (although it is critical of both).

📖 Acts 11:26

Epistles

👤 written by Pliny the Younger, a Roman governor (AD 61-113)

★ It references Christians worshipping Jesus.

📖 Acts 2:42-47

Annals

👤 written by Tacitus, a Roman historian (AD 116)

★ Refers to Jesus as Christ, the founder of Christianity, executed by Pontius Pilate under the reign of Tiberius.

📖 Luke 3:1-2

Jewish Antiquities

👤 written by Josephus, a Jewish historian (AD 93)

★ Calls James "the brother of Jesus, who is called Messiah" because Jesus was more famous than James.

📖 Matthew 13:55

Heel with Nail

⏳ 1968

★ Found in a bone box in a tomb, this find confirms both that crucifixion happened and that Jesus could have been buried in a tomb.

📖 Matthew 27:35,59-60

On the Lives of the Caesars

👤 written by Suetonius, a Roman historian (AD 120)

★ Talks about Jesus as an instigator of disturbances. Jesus wasn't really an instigator, but mobs formed against people who preached about Him.

📖 Acts 17:1-9

What's a bone box? See the **Ossuary of Caiaphas!**

Fishing Boat

⊗ 1986

★ Remember the story of Jesus and His 12 disciples on a ship? There was a storm, but Jesus calmed the wind and the waves.

▥ Luke 8:22-25

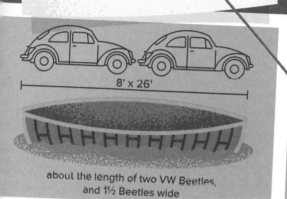

8' x 26'

about the length of two VW Beetles, and 1½ Beetles wide

The boat had seats for 12 passengers and an oarsman. The Guinness record for the most people crammed into a VW Beetle is 20!

Magdala Synagogue

⊗ 2009

★ Magdala is believed to be the birthplace of Mary Magdalene, the first eyewitness to Jesus's resurrection.

▥ John 20:11-18

Ossuary (Bone Box) of Caiaphas

⊗ 1990

★ The Gospels say Caiaphas was the Jewish high priest during Jesus's lifetime and was involved in Jesus's arrest.

▥ John 18:12-14

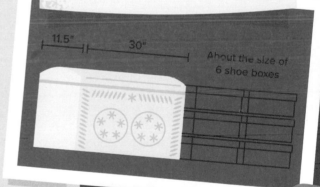

11.5"   30"

About the size of 6 shoe boxes

GALILEE

SEA OF GALILEE

JUDEA

JERUSALEM

HERODIUM

DEAD SEA

Ring with Pilate's Name

⊗ 1968-1969

★ It probably wasn't worn by Pilate himself but by someone who worked for him.

▥ Matthew 27:2

Why don't we have any of Jesus's stuff?

Maybe a favorite toy or a pair of sandals? Jesus was a humble Jewish carpenter. **What little He did have wouldn't have seemed important to preserve at the time.**

The very best evidence for Jesus's existence is something we can all see today: the spread of Christianity. In just about 2,000 years there are Christians in every country in the world. Think about it—could a Jewish carpenter from the first century have accomplished this feat on his own?

THE FOUR GOSPELS

or "GOOD NEWS"

The four Gospels give us the most well-known stories about Jesus.
Each Gospel gives us a deeper, more profound understanding of who Jesus is and what He did.

JESUS = KING

THE GOSPEL OF MATTHEW

MATTHEW 1:1

 Written by: the apostle Matthew

 Written for: Jews—people familiar with the Old Testament, the Law of Moses, and the prophets.

 Jesus is the promised King descended from David, the Anointed One (or Messiah). He fulfilled Old Testament hopes and prophecies.

 Refers to the Old Testament more than any other Gospel, including more than 130 Old Testament quotes and allusions!

 The only Gospel that mentions the magi at Jesus's birth.

Bridges the gap between the Old and New Testaments.
Matthew 5:17

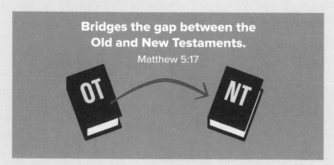

JESUS = SERVANT

THE GOSPEL OF MARK

MARK 10:45

 Written by: Mark the Evangelist, AKA "John, also called Mark," AKA John Mark.

Confused yet?

 Written for: Everyone (Jews and non-Jews).

 Jesus is the ultimate model of biblical service, demonstrated through all He did for us—particularly His miracles—not just what He said.

 The shortest, most action-packed Gospel! (And likely the oldest Gospel!)

 Mark assisted Peter and Paul. He likely used Peter's memories of Jesus for his Gospel.

Reads most like a story.
(This may have been intentional so it could be memorized and retold to others.)

WHY FOUR?

Well...Jesus was not your average joe.
He didn't just do ordinary things.

The four Gospel authors knew the importance of telling Jesus's story from **different perspectives** and painting distinct and accurate pictures of Jesus.

JESUS = SAVIOR

THE GOSPEL OF LUKE

LUKE 19:10

 Written by: Luke, the doctor

 Written for: Those who didn't know much about the life of Christ.

 Jesus is the long-awaited Messiah. A detailed account of His life showed that He came to seek and save the lost—all people, nations, and groups.

 The longest of the four Gospels and the longest book of the entire New Testament!

Because Luke goes into Jesus's story in such extensive detail!

Luke wrote the Gospel of Luke and the book of Acts. Together they make up about **27.5% of the New Testament.**

27.5%

NEW TESTAMENT

 Luke was also Paul's companion and probably had access to firsthand accounts of Jesus.

Luke didn't see Jesus's ministry firsthand.
He wrote his book based on the testimony of eyewitnesses.
Luke 1:1-4

JESUS = GOD

THE GOSPEL OF JOHN

JOHN 20:30-31

 Written by: John, "the disciple whom Jesus loved"

 Written for: Everyone!

 Jesus is the Word of God, the Son of God, and God Himself. Jesus's several "I am" statements (See pages 24-25) and many miraculous works proved He is God who came to save the world.

The story John tells begins much earlier than the other three—he begins with creation! (John 1:1)

 John also wrote other books in the New Testament: First, Second, and Third John and Revelation.

GOSPEL OF JOHN
FIRST JOHN
SECOND JOHN
THIRD JOHN
REVELATION

None of the Gospel writers try to chronicle Jesus's whole life.
John even tells us the world couldn't contain all the documentation of everything Jesus did!
John 21:25

Whoa!

17

HOMES

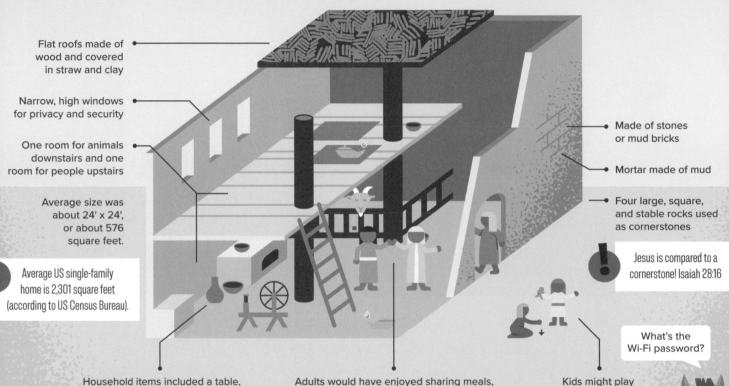

Flat roofs made of wood and covered in straw and clay

Narrow, high windows for privacy and security

One room for animals downstairs and one room for people upstairs

Average size was about 24' x 24', or about 576 square feet.

Average US single-family home is 2,301 square feet (according to US Census Bureau).

Made of stones or mud bricks

Mortar made of mud

Four large, square, and stable rocks used as cornerstones

Jesus is compared to a cornerstone! Isaiah 28:16

What's the Wi-Fi password?

Household items included a table, wooden bowls, olive oil lamp, and spinning wheel.

Adults would have enjoyed sharing meals, singing, storytelling, dancing, and maybe even board games (one resembling checkers!).

Kids might play with whistles, dolls, rattles, tops, etc.

FOOD

Staples included bread, olive oil, and local produce, like figs, olives, dates, and apples.

No individual plates—only shared dishes. For example, when Jesus told the disciples one of them would betray Him, He said, "The one who has dipped his hand into the bowl with me will betray me." Matthew 26:23

People sat on a mat near a table.

Goblets for wine

People also ate a lot of grains, like beans, peas, chickpeas, and lentils.

Anyone have a spare knife?

Meat was a luxury, but fish (fresh, dried, salted, smoked) and chicken were common.

Locusts were a delicacy.

No napkins or forks. Each person would have their own knife for cutting meat (BYOK), but generally they ate with their fingers. Servants might offer bowls of water for people to clean their hands during the meal.

THE WORLD DURI[NG]

LANGUAGE

Yaumo tobo
(Good day!)

Aramaic
Likely the primary language spoken by Jewish people, including Jesus.

Hallelujah
(praise the Lord)

Hebrew
Likely used only in the synagogue or when reading from the Torah.

Ya su
(hello)

Greek
Still a major influence in the area. The Romans and probably about 20% of the Jews in the area spoke Greek.

CLOTHING

Jewish Men

- dark, short hair
- trimmed beard
- knee-length tunic with a cloak
- tassels on the four corners of the cloak
- sandals

The second commandment warned against graven images, so there is very little artwork of Jewish people from that time.

Check out my tassels!

Jewish Women

- long, braided hair
- earrings
- head covering (likely the lower part of their faces would be covered too)
- bracelets
- ankle-length tunic with a cloak
- tassels on the four corners of the cloak
- anklets

JOBS

HERDING

FARMING

FISHING

CARPENTRY

TAILORING

MEDICINE

MILITARY/GOVERNMENT WORK

RELIGIOUS WORK

THE FOOTSTEPS OF JESUS

Jesus led an incredible life—full of preaching and teaching, 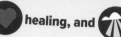 traveling, healing, and straight-up miracles!

FOLLOW ALONG IN HIS FOOTSTEPS. It's estimated that Jesus traveled more than...

...3,000 miles during His ministry.

That's like walking from **Seattle, WA**, to **Orlando, FL**.

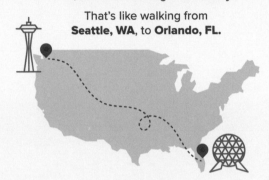

...20,000 miles during His lifetime.

That's like walking **80,000** trips around a track.

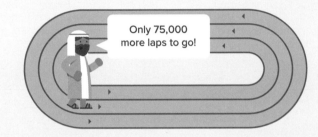

Only 75,000 more laps to go!

1
Is born.
Luke 2:10-20

2
Escapes from Herod.
Matthew 2:13-18

3
Returns with His family to Israel and grows up here.
Matthew 2:19-23

4
Is baptized by John the Baptist.
Matthew 3:13-17

5
Is tempted by Satan.*
Matthew 4:1-11

6
Performs His first miracle, turning water into wine.
John 2:1-11

7
Begins baptizing people.
John 3:22

8
Talks with a Samaritan woman at the well.
John 4:1-42

9
Heals an official's son.
John 4:46-54

10
Heals an invalid at a pool.
John 5:1-9

11
Preaches in His hometown, only to be rejected by His own people.
Luke 4:13-30

12
Establishes His preaching ministry (which is also a fulfillment of prophecy— see Isaiah 9:1-2).
Mark 1:14-15

13
Picks His 12 disciples and delivers the famous Sermon on the Mount.
Luke 6:12-49

14
Travels through Galilee, preaching, performing signs and miracles, and teaching in parables.
Luke 8:1-3

15
Calms a storm.
Mark 4:35-41

16
Heals a bleeding woman and two blind men, casts out demons, and brings a young girl back to life.
Matthew 9:18-35

17
Is rejected again.
Mark 6:1-6

18
Tours through this area preaching. During this time, John the Baptist is beheaded.
Mark 6:7-29

19
Feeds 5,000 men (plus women and children).
Matthew 14:13-21

20
Walks on water.
Matthew 14:22-33

21
Heals the daughter of a Syrophoenician woman.
Matthew 15:21-28

22
Heals many, including the lame, blind, and mute. Feeds 4,000 men (plus women and children).
Matthew 15:29-38

23
Begins teaching the disciples about His death and resurrection. Peter declares that Jesus is the Christ.
Luke 9:18-27

24
Is transfigured before Peter, James, and John (brother of James).*
Luke 9:28-36

25
Begins teaching the Jewish people who He is. They try to stone Him, but Jesus escapes.
John 7:14–8:59

26
Teaches in Mary and Martha's house.
Luke 10:38-42

27
Teaches about the kingdom of heaven and His upcoming death.
Luke 13:22–17:10

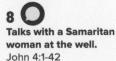

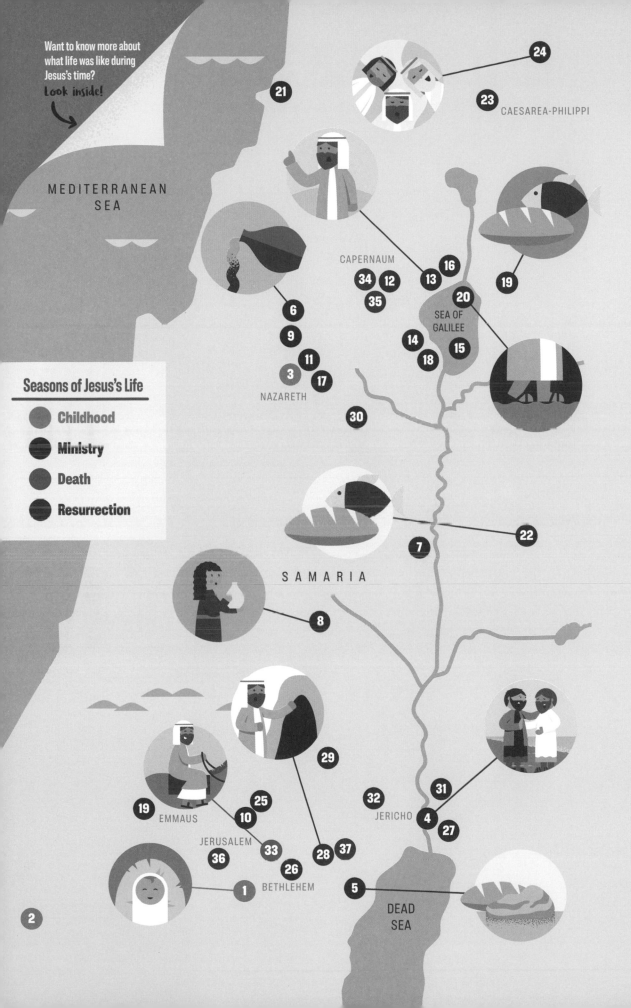

Want to know more about what life was like during Jesus's time?
Look inside!

MEDITERRANEAN SEA

CAESAREA-PHILIPPI

CAPERNAUM

SEA OF GALILEE

NAZARETH

Seasons of Jesus's Life

- Childhood
- Ministry
- Death
- Resurrection

SAMARIA

EMMAUS

JERUSALEM

BETHLEHEM

JERICHO

DEAD SEA

28 Raises Lazarus from the dead. Infuriated, the Pharisees plot to have Jesus killed.
John 11:1-53

29 Retreats with His disciples after hearing about a plot to kill Him.
John 11:53-54

30 Joins pilgrims heading to Jerusalem for Passover, healing and teaching along the way.
Luke 17:11–18:14

31 Connects with more followers, teaching about His death in Jerusalem for a third time.
Matthew 19:1–20:28

32 Heals a blind man and saves a tax collector named Zacchaeus.
Luke 18:35–19:10

33 Arrives in Jerusalem for what is now called Holy Week, is crucified, and rises from the dead.
Matthew 21:1–28:5

34 Appears to seven of His disciples while they were fishing and eats breakfast with them.
John 21

35 Appears to 11 of His disciples, giving them the Great Commission.
Matthew 28:16-20

36 Appears to His brother James and again to His disciples.
1 Corinthians 15:7; Luke 24:44-49

37 Ascends into heaven.
Luke 24:50-53

*Possible location, exact location is unknown.

19

THE TEMPLE

The temple during Jesus's time was the second temple (Solomon's temple was destroyed by the Babylonians).

This temple was rebuilt by Zerubbabel.

Herod the Great began renovating it in 20/19 BC.

Herod employed 10,000 masons and other craftsmen.

Herod employed 1,000 special Levites to work without disturbing the temple services.

64
Renovations completed around AD 64.

Destroyed completely in AD 70 by the Romans.

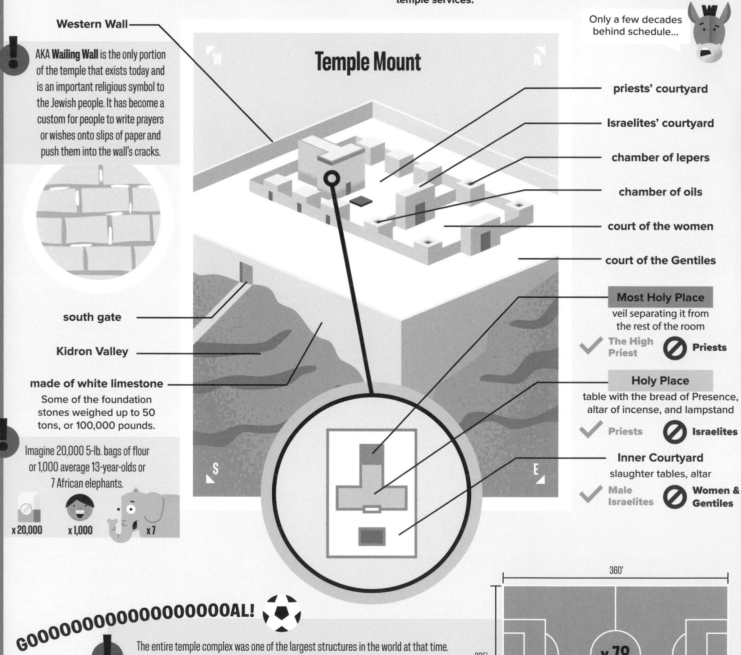

Western Wall

AKA **Wailing Wall** is the only portion of the temple that exists today and is an important religious symbol to the Jewish people. It has become a custom for people to write prayers or wishes onto slips of paper and push them into the wall's cracks.

Temple Mount

Only a few decades behind schedule...

priests' courtyard

Israelites' courtyard

chamber of lepers

chamber of oils

court of the women

court of the Gentiles

south gate

Kidron Valley

made of white limestone
Some of the foundation stones weighed up to 50 tons, or 100,000 pounds.

Imagine 20,000 5-lb. bags of flour or 1,000 average 13-year-olds or 7 African elephants.

x 20,000   x 1,000   x 7

Most Holy Place
veil separating it from the rest of the room
✓ The High Priest   🚫 Priests

Holy Place
table with the bread of Presence, altar of incense, and lampstand
✓ Priests   🚫 Israelites

Inner Courtyard
slaughter tables, altar
✓ Male Israelites   🚫 Women & Gentiles

GOOOOOOOOOOOOOOOOOOOOOOAL! ⚽

The entire temple complex was one of the largest structures in the world at that time. It was about 145 acres—that's about the size of 78 soccer fields!

360'

225'

x 78

MAJOR JEWISH FESTIVALS

PASSOVER

remembers God sparing the firstborn of Israel and bringing them out of slavery in Egypt

 Jesus was sacrificed as the perfect Passover Lamb

UNLEAVENED BREAD

remembers the Exodus from Egypt and years in the desert

 burial of Jesus, the Bread of Life

8 DAYS IN MARCH/APRIL

FIRSTFRUITS

beginning of harvest, dedicating that harvest to God

resurrection of Jesus

FEAST OF WEEKS OR PENTECOST

end of harvest, gratitude given to God

 Holy Spirit is given, and the harvest began with 3,000 people

 50 DAYS AFTER PASSOVER

PURIM

remembers God protecting the Jewish people from Haman and the Persian Empire

 God keeps His promises, including sending a Messiah

 LATE WINTER/EARLY SPRING

FESTIVAL OF LIGHTS (HANUKKAH)

celebrates the dedication of the second temple

 Jesus is the eternal light of the world

 WINTER

HEBREW CALENDAR

SPRING
APR
MAR
MAY
FEB
JUNE
JAN
SUMMER
JULY
WINTER
DEC
AUG
NOV
SEP
OCT
AUTUMN

SABBATH

resting like God did after creating the world, trusting in God for provision

 Jesus's sufficient work on the cross, our future rest in the coming kingdom

 EVERY SATURDAY

FEAST OF TABERNACLES OR BOOTHS

God's protection and deliverance during the 40 years in the wilderness

 Jesus will return, live among His people, and reign eternally.

DAY OF ATONEMENT

the high priest atoned for the people's sin

 Jesus's sacrifice on the cross atoned for the sins of the world.

FEAST OF TRUMPETS

end of one agricultural year and beginning of the next

 the promised return of Jesus

 21 DAYS IN THE FALL

JESUS'S SEVEN I AM STATEMENTS

When someone says, **"I am…"** they reveal something about themselves. Jesus saying "I am…" tells us something very important about Him: He is God, the great I AM (Exodus 3:14). Jesus talks not only about **what** He can do or give, but also about **who** He is.

I am the BREAD OF LIFE John 6:35

God had miraculously provided **bread** in the desert for the Israelites and called it "manna."

Manna means "What is it?" in Hebrew. It is also known as the "bread of heaven."

Bread can fill us up, but we will get hungry again.

Jesus **fills and sustains our souls** and satisfies our hunger for more.
John 6:51

The largest loaf of bread was made in 2008 by Joaquim Gonçalves in Brazil, weighing 3,463.46 lbs.

I am the TRUE VINE John 15:5

Grapevines and vineyards are mentioned in the Bible over 500 times! They symbolize something blessed, good, and prosperous.

Disconnected from the vine, branches bear no fruit.

Disconnected from Jesus, we bear **no spiritual fruit.**

Isaiah compared Israel to a vineyard that produced only **bad fruit.**
Isaiah 5

Connected to the vine, branches bear fruit and thrive.

Connected to Jesus, we bear **spiritual fruit** and thrive.

Jesus fulfills Israel's destiny as the vine that produces life and fruit.
Psalm 80:4-17

BRANCHES = US **VINE** = JESUS **FRUIT** = LOVE, JOY, PEACE… (GALATIANS 5:22-23)

I am the LIGHT OF THE WORLD John 8:12

In the beginning, God said, **"Let there be light."**
Genesis 1:3

God led the people of Israel by a **pillar of blazing fire.**
Exodus 13–14

God dwells in **"unapproachable light."**
1 Timothy 6:16

John refers to Jesus as **the light.**
John 1:4-14

NASA scientists found that without gravity, a flame becomes spherical!

Jesus provides **spiritual light** for anyone who follows Him.

During biblical times, traditional candles hadn't been invented yet. Instead, there were lamps, typically made of pottery, with a linen wick, which burned olive or other oil.

I am the **GOOD SHEPHERD** John 10:11

God promised that He would shepherd his people.
Ezekiel 34:11-16

Good shepherds lead their sheep, guide them, and keep them from wandering. **They will sacrifice everything for their flock.**

Jesus is the true and **good shepherd**. He leads us, guides us, and keeps us from wandering into sin. **He sacrificed His life for ours.**

When **sheep** enter through the **gate**, they become the shepherd's **treasured sheep**.

When **you** enter through **Jesus**, you become one of God's **treasured children**.

! Sheep were often kept in a sheepfold, a rough circle of rocks that formed a wall. **Shepherds would literally become a gate**, laying across the small opening to the sheepfold! This kept sheep in and safe from harm.

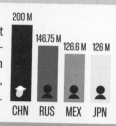

! China has the most sheep in the world—more than the human populations of Russia, Mexico, and Japan.

200 M	146.75 M	126.6 M	126 M
CHN	RUS	MEX	JPN

THE SHEPHERD = GOD   **THE SHEEP** = GOD'S CHILDREN   **THE GATE** = JESUS

I am the **GATE FOR THE SHEEP** John 10:7
I am the **WAY** and the **TRUTH** and the **LIFE** John 14:6

Jesus is **the only way** to the Father.

Jesus is the full truth (revelation) of the **Father**.

! Twice in the book of Acts, Christians are called **"followers of the Way."** Paul said that he "persecuted followers of this Way" (Acts 22:4) until he too became a "follower of the Way" (Acts 24:14).

Jesus is the **way** to eternal **Life**.

I am the **RESURRECTION** and the **LIFE** John 11:25

The power of **resurrection** is only found in Jesus.

Jesus is the **master over death** itself.

Jesus promises **eternal life** to all who believe in Him.

Those who believe in Jesus will experience a **bodily resurrection** when Jesus returns.

The BiRTH of JESUS
THE WHOLE BIBLE HAS LED UP TO THIS MOMENT.

 **Do not be afraid.**

 Angels often serve God as messengers. Notice how often they showed up around the birth of Jesus!

Do not be afraid.

Do not be afraid.

ELIZABETH   ZECHARIAH   JOHN THE BAPTIST JESUS   MARY   JOSEPH

John the Baptist came to prepare the people for Jesus. Look at how their birth stories compare in Luke 1 and 2.

 GABRIEL ANNOUNCES THEIR BIRTH

 GABRIEL GIVES THEIR NAMES

 GABRIEL TELLS WHAT THEIR MINISTRY WILL BE

 MOMS GIVE GLORY TO GOD

 BIRTHS ARE MIRACULOUS

 NAMED ON THE EIGHTH DAY

 PEOPLE ARE FILLED WITH WONDER BY THEIR BIRTH

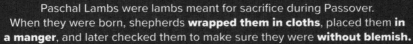

  "A Savior has been born to you; he is the Messiah, the Lord. This will be a sign to you: You will find a baby **wrapped in cloths** and **lying in a manger**."
Luke 2:11-12

The shepherds would have understood better than anyone the significance of the angel's words.

Paschal Lambs were lambs meant for sacrifice during Passover. When they were born, shepherds **wrapped them in cloths**, placed them **in a manger**, and later checked them to make sure they were **without blemish**.

Placing Jesus in a manger pointed forward to how Jesus would be the sinless, blameless, and **unblemished** Lamb who was sacrificed for our sin.

God called the nation of Israel His son (Exodus 4:22). Jesus is the faithful, true, and righteous Son of God. Look at how **Jesus's** journey parallels the **Israelites'**.

 JESUS

 ISRAELITES

Herod orders all boys under the age of two to be killed.

Pharaoh orders all Hebrew boys to be killed.

Take Mary and Jesus to Egypt.

Mary and Joseph save Jesus by taking Him to Egypt.

Moses's mom saves him by hiding him in Egypt.

Jesus leaves Egypt.

Israel escapes from Egypt in the Exodus.

Matthew tells of Jesus's return from Egypt and then His baptism in the Jordan.*

The Israelites were "baptized" as they escaped through the sea (1 Corinthians 10:2).

Jesus spends 40 days and 40 nights fasting before being tempted.*

The Israelites wander in the desert for 40 years.

*More on these events on pages 28 and 30.

God made him who had no sin to be sin for us, so that in him we might become the righteousness of God.
2 Corinthians 5:21

Hint: *Him* is Jesus!

JESUS IS BAPTIZED

Matthew 3:13

Matthew continues to show us how Jesus's journey parallels the Israelites' journey (see page 27). After Jesus and His family returned from Egypt to live in Nazareth, Matthew next describes Jesus's baptism in the Jordan River.

> This is my Son, whom I love; with him I am well pleased.
> Matthew 3:17

> I need to be baptized by you, and do you come to me?
> Matthew 3:14

> Let it be so now; it is proper for us to do this to fulfill all righteousness.
> Matthew 3:15

When Jesus came out of the water, heaven opened, and the Spirit of God descended on Him like a dove.
Matthew 3:16

John the Baptist (aka JB)

Prepared the way for Jesus by preaching in the wilderness, calling people to repent of their sins and to be baptized

Ate locusts and honey

Dressed like the prophet Elijah
2 Kings 1:8

Wore clothes of camel hair (comfy!) and a leather belt

Jesus (aka JC)

Savior, Messiah, and an all-around good guy

An adult by this time

Wore a seamless tunic and sandals

Jordan River

Eww, locusts?
Locusts are still eaten today. Often they are salted and dried, cooked, pounded, or fried in butter, tasting like shrimp.

ALL THREE MEMBERS OF THE TRINITY WERE PRESENT...

The Father

The Son

The Spirit

After Jesus was baptized, He (or His disciples) began baptizing people as well.

Jesus instructed the disciples to make disciples of all nations, baptizing them in the name of the **Father**, **Son**, and **Holy Spirit**.

Matthew 28:19

WHY DO WE GET BAPTIZED?

To follow Jesus's faithful example.

To publicly declare our faith in Jesus.

To demonstrate our repentance (turning from sin).

our death to sin   our rebirth in Christ

Whoa! Jesus's baptism in the Jordan River marked the start of His ministry, just like the Israelites crossing the same river led them to the Promised Land (Joshua 3:14-17).

JESUS IS TEMPTED

After His baptism, Jesus was led by the Holy Spirit to the wilderness to **fast for 40 days** and then to **be tempted** (or tested). Satan tried to tempt Jesus to ruin God's plan for saving the world. If Jesus had sinned, He wouldn't have been able to save us from our sin.

"If you are the Son of God, tell these stones to become bread."
Matthew 4:3

Satan wanted Jesus to give in to His human needs. Remember, Jesus had just fasted for 40 days, and He would have been HUNGRY!

"Man does not live on bread alone but on every word that comes from the mouth of the Lord."
Deuteronomy 8:3

FASTING VS. "FAST EATING"

fasting: to choose not to eat

The average person can survive 1 or 2 months without food but only about 3 days without water. (Don't worry, Jesus drank water.)

fast eating: competitive eating or speed eating

In 2019, Leah Shutkever set a Guinness World Record by eating a burrito in 35.26 seconds.

"If you are the Son of God . . . throw yourself down."
Matthew 4:5-6

Satan wanted Jesus to act prideful and show that He could command the angels.

"Do not put the Lord your God to the test."
Deuteronomy 6:16

HOW FAR DID SATAN ASK JESUS TO FALL?

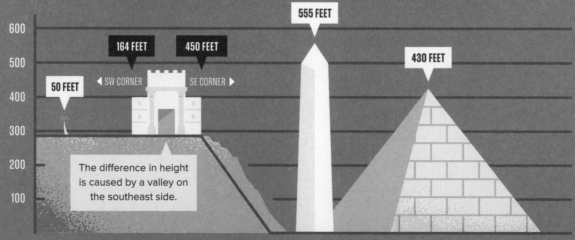

The difference in height is caused by a valley on the southeast side.

50 FEET — AVERAGE PALM TREE
164 FEET — SW CORNER / 450 FEET — SE CORNER — THE TEMPLE
555 FEET — WASHINGTON MONUMENT
430 FEET — GREAT PYRAMID

> ## "All this I will give you...if you will bow down and worship me."
> **Matthew 4:9**

Satan wanted Jesus to show a desire for wealth and power that would "surpass" God's (impossible!) without having to die on the cross.

> ## "Fear the LORD your God, serve him only and take your oaths in his name."
> **Deuteronomy 6:13**

THE LORD

JESUS IS OBEDIENT TO GOD.

He responds to each of Satan's temptations by quoting from Deuteronomy.
By doing this, Jesus is connecting His **40 days** of testing to the Israelites' **40 years** in the desert.

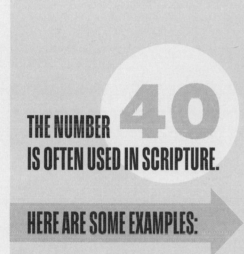

THE NUMBER 40 IS OFTEN USED IN SCRIPTURE.

HERE ARE SOME EXAMPLES:

40 Days...

Jesus's days of testing
Matthew 4

Jesus's post-resurrection appearances
Acts 1:3

Noah's flood
Genesis 7:12

Jonah's warning
Jonah 3:4

40 Years...

Israelites' wandering in the desert
Deuteronomy 8:2

Moses's exile in Midian
Acts 7:29-30

King David's reign
2 Samuel 5:4

King Solomon's reign
1 Kings 11:42

WHAT THREE LESSONS CAN WE LEARN?

1 MEMORIZE SCRIPTURE

Jesus used God's Word to resist temptation.

2 READ THE BIBLE

Satan quoted Scripture, but Jesus understood the words' true meaning.

3 OBEY GOD'S WORD

Jesus trusted God above all other influences, avoiding temptation.

THE LAMB OF GOD

THE PASSOVER LAMB

God cared about His people in slavery, so He sent ten plagues to deliver them from the Egyptians. The tenth plague killed every firstborn son, but God protected those who sacrificed a lamb (the Passover Lamb) and spread the blood across the doorposts of their homes.

WHY A LAMB?

In the Old Testament, people sacrificed animals so their sins could be forgiven.

An animal sacrifice? I'm outta here—tell people I'm on the lam!

THE PASSOVER CELEBRATION

Every year, Jews celebrate their deliverance with a Passover feast.

THE PASSOVER LAMB

A lamb (without defect), roasted and served with bitter herbs (maror) and a sweet apple mixture (kharoset).

The bitter herbs symbolize the bitterness of the people's slavery, and the sweet apple mixture represents the sweet promise of God's redemption.

MATZAH

Bread made without yeast.

The matzah is broken in two, representing the rush to leave Egypt before the bread could rise.

Half of the matzah is wrapped in cloth and hidden away, called the "afikomen" or "the Coming One."

1 THE CUP OF SALVATION

Symbolizes God bringing Israel out of slavery and setting His people apart.

2 THE CUP OF JUDGMENT

A reminder that plagues are THE WORST and that God walks with His people through hard times.

3 THE CUP OF REDEMPTION

A reminder that the people were redeemed from slavery.

4 THE CUP OF PRAISE

A reminder that God blesses.

JESUS IS THE LAMB OF GOD

Symbolizes that we are God's chosen people.

Symbolizes Christ's perfect sacrifice for the sins of the world.

Jesus was without defect.

Jesus was given wine vinegar on the cross.

Symbolizes Christ's body, broken on the cross.
Luke 22:19

Jesus was wrapped in cloths and hidden away in the tomb.

Jesus is the Coming One!

Symbolizes His blood that was spilled on the cross.
Luke 22:20

This cup is the blood of the New Covenant. See page 11.

Symbolizes the freedom we have in Jesus, the Messiah.

Symbolizes our praise as we unite with Jesus in paradise.

Look, the Lamb of God, who takes away the sin of the world.
John 1:29

THE LAMB REIGNS

In Revelation 5:1-12, John sees heaven...

The scroll holds all the truth about the Messiah and the coming kingdom. But John is told that no one can open it except the Lion of the tribe of Judah.

Genesis 49:8-10

Expecting to see a powerful, mighty lion, John instead sees a slain Lamb.

The gentle Lamb of God was able to open the scroll.

Heaven erupts in song, "Worthy is the Lamb who was slain, to receive power and wealth and wisdom and strength and honor and glory and praise!"

The Israelites expected the Messiah to be a mighty king, riding in on a horse! Instead, He was a humble man who entered Jerusalem on a [ahem] donkey.

Psst. I'm back. Remember, David descended from the royal line of Judah!

Jesus is due all praise and glory for being the final sacrifice—the humble Lamb— who took away the sins of the world so we may be forgiven.

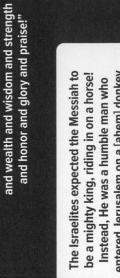

MIND-BLOWING MIRACLES

Jesus performed amazing miracles during His life,
and only a fraction of them are included in the Bible (John 21:25).
These supernatural acts of love and power revealed profound things about Jesus.

JESUS'S MIRACLES...

| Validate Jesus's claims about Himself and His teachings | Remind us of Jesus's power and authority over evil | Show Jesus's unending love and compassion for us | Provide hope when we pray or need a miracle | Reflect the close relationship Jesus wants with us |

JESUS HEALED

Jesus healed lots of people. He cured people of diseases, paralysis, blindness, deafness, and much more!

Ephphatha!
(Be opened!)

A Deaf Man with Difficulty Speaking • Mark 7:31-37

People from the Decapolis brought Jesus a deaf and mute man. Jesus touched the man's ears and put His own saliva on the man's tongue, opening his ears and releasing his tongue to speak plainly!

> Jesus healed deafness completely, but people have been helping those hard of hearing for a long time! The first attempt to use electricity to aid hearing was in 1790, and the first electrical hearing aid was invented in 1892!

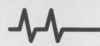

A centurion's dying servant
Matthew 8:5-13

A bleeding woman
Matthew 9:18-26

JESUS SHOWED HIS POWER OVER NATURE

Jesus wasn't showing off; He was helping people believe He is the Son of God.

Walking on Water • Mark 7:31-37

Jesus told the disciples to get into a boat and travel ahead of Him. That night, Jesus was praying on a mountainside alone, and the boat was quite far away, rocked by waves and strong winds. Shortly before dawn, Jesus walked out on the lake to them.

Peter doubted it was Jesus at first but said he'd walk out on the water to Jesus if it was Him. Peter tried and became fearful. Jesus caught him and said "You of little faith. Why did you doubt?" They climbed into the boat, and the wind died down.

Take courage! It is I. Don't be afraid.

> DON'T TRY THIS AT HOME! Or at the lake. Or river. Or any body of water, really.
>
> Not to make waves, but no one can walk on water except Jesus! Or you could have a miraculous, personal encounter like Peter did.
>
> Most of us would have to run about 67 mph just to have a chance!

Calming the storm
Luke 8:22-25

Withering the fig tree
Matthew 21:18-22

JESUS CAST OUT EVIL SPIRITS

Jesus proved He had full authority over evil by casting out many demons.

If it is by the Spirit of God that I drive out demons, then the kingdom of God has come upon you.

Beelzebul • Matthew 12:22-28

Jesus was brought a demon-possessed man who was blind and mute. Jesus healed him so he could talk and see!

The synoptic Gospels contain more than 60 stories and references to demon possession and exorcisms. The first recorded miracle in Mark (1:21-27) is the excorcism in the synagogue. In fact, in the first half of Mark's Gospel, the only ones on earth who know the identity of Jesus are demons!

In a synagogue
Mark 1:21-27

Near some tombs
Matthew 8:28-34

JESUS PROVIDED FOR PEOPLE'S NEEDS

Jesus provided for people in amazing ways. He turned water into wine, fed thousands of people, and provided great hauls of fish.

Fill the jars with water, draw some out, and take it to the master of the feast.

Turns Water into Wine • John 2:1-11

Jesus and His disciples had been invited to a wedding at Cana in Galilee. Jesus's mother let Him know that they had run out of wine at the wedding. He then turned the water in six stone water jars, the kind used by the Jews for ceremonial washing, into wine.

The water jars could hold 20 to 30 gallons each!

That would be like **3,840 JUICE BOXES** =

Feeds five thousand
Luke 9:10-17

Supplies a big catch
Luke 5:1-11

JESUS SHOWED HIS POWER OVER DEATH

By raising others from death and being resurrected Himself, Jesus confirmed that He is God. Only He could conquer death itself!

Raising Lazarus from the Dead • John 11:1-44

I am the resurrection and the life.

Jesus's friend Lazarus was sick. After assuring Lazarus's sisters that his sickness wouldn't end in death, Jesus found that Lazarus had been placed in a tomb for four days. Jesus comforted the sisters and reassured them that Lazarus would rise again. They went to the tomb, where Jesus called for Lazarus to come out, and Lazarus emerged alive!

The Bible tells of several resurrections—three individuals in the Old Testament and five individuals in the New Testament. An unspecified number of people are mentioned following Jesus's resurrection (Matthew 27:50-53). In every case, each person lived again but also died again...except for Jesus!

Jesus is resurrected
Luke 24:6-7
(See page 49)

Jesus raisies the widow's son
Luke 7:11-18

SERMON ON THE MOUNT

Matthew 5–7 records an epic teaching of Jesus called the Sermon on the Mount (because Jesus taught it from a mountain).

The BEATITUDES

Matthew 5:3-12

Jesus paints a big-picture view of what life is like in God's kingdom.

BLESSED ARE...	FOR...
The poor in spirit	Theirs is the kingdom of heaven
The meek	They will inherit the earth
The merciful	They will be shown mercy
The peacemakers	They will be called children of God
You when you are insulted because of Jesus	Your reward in heaven is great

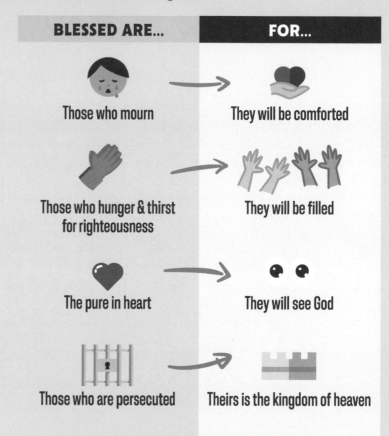

BLESSED ARE...	FOR...
Those who mourn	They will be comforted
Those who hunger & thirst for righteousness	They will be filled
The pure in heart	They will see God
Those who are persecuted	Theirs is the kingdom of heaven

EXPECTATIONS for the COMMANDMENTS

God cares about our hearts just as much as our actions.   Matthew 5:21-47

Do not murder.
Do not be angry.
Being angry or calling someone a fool is **as wrong as** murder.

Do not break your oath.
Do not make an oath at all.
We shouldn't make promises we **might not be able to keep.**

An eye for an eye, a tooth for a tooth.
Turn the other cheek.
We should **never seek revenge,** even if we think the other person deserves it.

Love your neighbor.
Love your enemy.
We should love those who like us **and** those who don't like us.

FALSE SPIRITUALITY

Be careful not to show off how spiritual you are.

 Show off how generous you are.

 Give in secret.

| Show off how well you pray.

 Pray in secret.

| Show off how miserable you are when you fast.

 Fast in secret.

THE LORD'S PRAYER

Jesus gives us a sample prayer, which we call the Lord's Prayer.

Our Father in heaven, ——— We can pray confidently, knowing **God is a loving Father** who wants to help us.

hallowed be your name, ——— "Hallowed" means **"set apart."** We want to remember that God is not like anyone else. He is greater than all of creation.

your kingdom come, your will be done, on earth as it is in heaven. ——— Prayer is not about trying to get God to do what we want, but about us **wanting to do what He wants.**

Give us today our daily bread. ——— God wants us to ask Him to help us with our **daily problems.**

And forgive us our debts, as we also have forgiven our debtors. ——— We need to confess our sins to God and ask for **forgiveness**, remembering to forgive others as well.

And lead us not into temptation, but deliver us from the evil one. ——— We need to ask God to **help us not to sin** and to protect us from Satan.

IT'S NOT ABOUT THE MONEY

If we are spiritual, will God make us rich? It doesn't work that way.

We shouldn't seek riches on earth, but in heaven.

You can't love both God and money.

We don't need to worry about money, because God will take care of us.

Seek the kingdom first, and God will take care of your needs.

JUDGE NOT

Drawing attention to other people's mistakes is rarely helpful.

We will be judged the same way we judge others.

 Rather than worry about the **speck** in someone else's eye, we should take the **log** out of our eye.

We should treat people the way we want to be treated.

This is called "**the golden rule**" (even though Jesus doesn't use that term) because it is an easy and important way to remember how to treat other people.

THE PARABLES

Parable (n.): A short story that teaches an important lesson.

PARABLES are like cakes. They have multiple (delicious) layers.

← STORY

MEANING

← APPLICATION

WHY DID JESUS TEACH IN PARABLES? MATTHEW 13:10-17

TO HIDE THE TRUTH...
from people who thought they were too smart to learn from Jesus.

TO TEACH THE TRUTH...
to people who wanted to learn from Jesus.

WISE AND FOOLISH BUILDERS

Matthew 7:24-27; Luke 6:47-49

A **wise** man builds his **house on rock,** and it withstands the flood.

A **foolish** man builds his **house on sand,** and it crumbles in the flood.

HOUSE ON ROCK =
the person who hears Jesus's words and **OBEYS** them

STORM =
judgment

HOUSE ON SAND =
the person who hears Jesus's words and **DOESN'T OBEY** them

The **sand** on the shore of the Sea of Galilee was hard when dry and would give the impression of being solid and strong. But rain storms would prove the sand was an unreliable surface.

So **wise** builders dug well below the surface of the sand to find bedrock to use as a foundation.

10'

WHEN WE HEAR AND OBEY JESUS'S WORDS, WE ARE ABLE TO WITHSTAND ANY STORM THAT COMES OUR WAY.

MUSTARD SEED

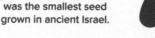

Matthew 13:31-32; Mark 4:30-32; Luke 13:18-19

A **mustard seed** is extremely tiny, but after it is planted, it grows very fast.

MUSTARD SEED =
the kingdom of God

The mustard seed was the smallest seed grown in ancient Israel.

← mustard seed
← apple seed
← orchid seed

The **kingdom of God** would start very small, but it would grow faster than anyone could ever imagine.

In just a few months, a mustard plant can grow over 10' tall. Imagine if you grew that fast!

Jesus promised, "I will build my church."
Matthew 16:18

NO MATTER WHAT HAPPENS, WE CAN KNOW THAT THE GOSPEL WILL CONTINUE TO CHANGE LIVES.

HOW MANY PARABLES ARE IN THE GOSPELS?

There are parables in the Old Testament too! Check these out: Jeremiah 18:1-10; Ezekiel 17

UNIQUE ACCOUNTS

- **MATTHEW** (11)
- **MARK** (2)
- **LUKE** (16)
- **JOHN** (There are no parables recorded in the Gospel of John)

SHARED ACCOUNTS (9)

These are the same parables shared in multiple Gospel accounts

---

GOOD SAMARITAN
Luke 10:29-37

A man is beaten along a **road** by robbers. After being ignored by a **priest and a Levite**, he is rescued by an unlikely hero—a **Samaritan**.

SAMARITAN =	PRIEST & LEVITE =	ROAD =
a foreigner who was hated by the Israelites.	religious leaders who were supposed to be the most righteous people, but even they were not willing to help.	a dangerous 17-mile journey with a steep and windy road where robbers waited for travelers.

Yet he was willing to help someone who didn't like him.

The **Samaritan** poured **oil** and **wine** on the wounds.

Olive oil was used medicinally

Wine was used to disinfect wounds

The **Samaritan** paid **two denarii** to the innkeeper to care for victim.

 1 DENARIUS = 1 DAY'S WAGE

WE SHOULD LOVE EVERYONE AROUND US, EVEN IF THEY ARE NOT KIND TO US.

PRODIGAL SON
Luke 15:11-32

A **son** takes his father's money and abandons his family. After spending all his **inheritance**, he returns and is joyfully accepted by his **father**.

LOST SON =	FATHER =
people who are not following God	God
Inheritance (n.): share of a father's wealth that a son would receive upon the father's death.	Runs to greet his son. In that time, fathers usually walked slowly to appear dignified.
Asking for the inheritance early is like saying, "I wish you were dead."	This shows how excited he was to see his lost son.

The lost son was given the best **robe**, a **ring**, **sandals**, and a **party**.

 ROBE = honor

 RING = the father's authority

 SANDALS = the son's acceptance into the family again

 PARTY = where a fattened calf was served

Calves were usually cooked only for large events, like weddings. This means the whole village may have been invited to join in the celebration of the son's return.

NO MATTER WHAT, YOU CAN ALWAYS COME BACK TO GOD, AND HE WILL JOYFULLY ACCEPT YOU.

DISCIPLES BY THE DOZEN

The twelve **disciples** (also called **apostles**), or **"THE TWELVE"** (not a bad superhero team name!), were Jesus's closest followers and leaders in the movement that became Christianity.

HOW TO RECRUIT A DISCIPLE

PHASE 1: A CALL TO FOLLOW
Matthew 4:19; Luke 5:11; John 1:35-51

PHASE 2: A CALL TO LEARN
Luke 11:1-11

PHASE 3: A CALL TO MINISTRY
Matthew 10:1-4; Luke 6:12-16

THE OG 6

PETER
Son of Jonah

Cephas · Simon · Peter

 Not the one who was swallowed by a big fish.

JAMES
Son of Zebedee

One of the **sons of thunder**

James the Greater · James

JOHN
James's brother

One of the **sons of thunder**

The "inner circle" of disciples.
These three witnessed miracles and moments other apostles didn't:

JESUS RAISING JAIRUS'S DAUGHTER

JESUS'S TRANSFIGURATION

JESUS'S VIGIL IN GETHSEMANE

ANDREW
Peter's brother

The first disciple Jesus called in the Gospel of John

PHILIP
The apostle

Mentioned 8 times in the New Testament. The early church often mixed up Philip the apostle and Philip the evangelist. Totally different guys.

BARTHOLOMEW
Associated with Philip

 This may be the same person as Nathaniel from John 1:43-51.

THE **TAX MAN**

MATTHEW

Was called sometime after the first six

He was a tax collector.

Matthew **Levi**

Kids, tax collectors weren't very nice.

Tax collectors overcharged people to make themselves rich. Matthew invited other tax gatherers and lowlifes to dinner with Jesus—probably because they were Matthew's only friends.

Go Fish!
Many of the disciples, including Peter, were fishermen.

Fishing . . . for Fish
An important part of the first-century Galilee economy. "Musht," a type of carp, are often 15 inches long and about 3 pounds.

Fishing . . . for Men
When Jesus called Peter, Andrew, James, and John, they were fishing with nets (Matthew 4:18-22).

What's in a Name?
In New Testament times, many people had a Jewish (**Hebrew**) name and a <u>Greek</u> name.

Like **Simon Peter**!

Peter **Cephas** **Simon**

THE **REST...**

THOMAS

Famous for doubting

No doubt; He wasn't given a real name in the Bible manuscripts. "Thomas" comes from the Aramaic word **tě'omâ**, which means "twin." Most manuscripts include the description "called Didymus," or "called the Twin."

SIMON

The Zealot

Zealots were Jewish extremists who wanted to overthrow Rome.

JUDAS

Son of James

Judas **Thaddeus**

JAMES

Son of Alphaeus

JUDAS ISCARIOT

Oversaw the group's money. Infamously betrayed Jesus for 30 pieces of silver. Yikes, he wasn't super trustworthy. (John 12:4-6)

The New Guy

MATTHIAS

Added to the 11 apostles after Judas died. And that's about all we know.

WHOOPS-A-DAISY DISCIPLES: DOUBTS, DENIALS, AND…"DUDE?!"

The Gospels show us that the disciples were truly human—sometimes slow learners and a bit spiritually dense.

Luke 24:25

PETER

doubted and started to sink when he walked on the water to Jesus

rebuked Jesus when He spoke of His coming death

denied Jesus

JAMES AND JOHN

asked Jesus if they should call down fire from heaven to destroy a Samaritan village (Whoa.) Luke 9:54

wanted to sit at Jesus's left and right in His kingdom

THOMAS

doubted the reports about Jesus's resurrection

JUDAS ISCARIOT

stole money that was donated to Jesus's ministry

betrayed Jesus

JESUS'S OPPONENTS

Jesus had many followers and people who loved Him, but many other people tried to stop Him and His ministry.
Some of His opponents were close to Him, some were religious, some were from the government, and some were even cosmic enemies.

JESUS'S FAMILY
Jesus's brothers and other family members.
They tried to seize Jesus because they thought He was crazy.

Mark 3:20-21

Jesus said that His true family are those who obey God. Mark 3:35

 At least two of His brothers ended up believing in Jesus after the resurrection (James and Jude). They each wrote a book in the New Testament.

JUDAS
One of Jesus's 12 disciples.
He allowed Satan to control him (John 13:27), and he betrayed Jesus for 30 pieces of silver.

Matthew 26:14-16

Jesus knew that Judas had betrayed Him, but He still washed Judas's feet and served him at the Last Supper.

He handled the money for Jesus and the disciples (John 12:6).

Because people had to walk everywhere, their feet got really really dirty and stinky. A gracious host would usually have a servant wash their guest's feet.

PEOPLE OF NAZARETH
People who knew Him since He was a little boy.
When Jesus told them He was the Messiah, they didn't believe Him, and they tried to throw Him off a cliff! (Yikes!)

Luke 4:16-30

Jesus stopped doing miracles in Nazareth because they didn't believe in Him.

SCRIBES
Experts in the Old Testament Law.
They claimed that Jesus was possessed by Satan, questioned His teachings and tried to trick Jesus, and conspired to have Jesus arrested.

Mark 12:28-40

Jesus warned the people about the hypocrisy of the scribes.

Because printers weren't invented yet, scribes handwrote the Bible to make copies.

PHARISEES
Teachers of the Old Testament Law.
They constantly criticized Jesus and His disciples for not following their interpretation of the Law, especially in regard to the Sabbath.

Matthew 12:1-14

Jesus rebuked the Pharisees for their hypocrisy.

The apostle Paul was a Pharisee before he became a Christian.

hypocrite (n): person who pretends to be one way but acts the total opposite.

Jesus saw through their tricks and answered their questions by using Scripture from the Law.

Jesus's parents, Joseph and Mary, fled to Egypt to escape from Herod. They stayed in Egypt until after Herod died.

Jesus remained silent before Herod.

My kingdom is in heaven.

Jesus told Pilate that He was not a threat to Roman rule because His kingdom was a heavenly kingdom, not an earthly kingdom.

Jesus cast demons out of the people.

Jesus resisted Satan's temptation and did not sin.

SADDUCEES
Luke 20:27-40

The ruling class in Judea at the time of Jesus.
They tried to trick Jesus by asking Him questions. They conspired to have Jesus arrested and killed.

They did not believe in the resurrection and believed that only Genesis–Deuteronomy (the Law) should be included in the Bible.

KING HEROD THE GREAT
Matthew 2:1-13

King of Judea when Jesus was born.
When he learned that a king was born in Bethlehem, he had all the baby boys in Bethlehem killed.

KING HEROD ANTIPAS
Luke 23:6-12

King of Galilee when Jesus was an adult.
He wanted Jesus to perform a miracle at His trial. He mocked Jesus and sent Him back to Pilate.

Son of Herod the Great.

PILATE
John 19:1-16

Governor of Judea when Jesus was an adult.
After the Jews turned Jesus over to the Romans, he oversaw His trial and sentenced Him to be crucified.

DEMONS
Luke 23:6-12

Fallen angels who followed Satan when he rebelled against God.
They lived inside the bodies of people to torment them. When they met Jesus, they recognized Him as the Son of God and were terrified.

SATAN
Matthew 4:1-11

A fallen angel who rebelled against God.
After Jesus had fasted for 40 days in the wilderness, Satan tempted Jesus to sin by telling Him he would give Him all the kingdoms of the world if He would bow down and worship him.

JESUS LOVED

Jesus loved everyone and went out of His way to care for those who were **considered unimportant by society**.

 KIDS in that day were seen as annoyances (not nice!), but Jesus honored children. He wanted children to be with Him and pointed to them as examples of faith and humility.

! John 6:9 mentions the boy who had five loaves and two small fish. (Yum!)

Jesus fed five thousand men with **one boy's** food.

Mark 6:30-44

Don't worry, the boy got some too.

In desperation, **a woman** reached out and touched Jesus's cloak. Jesus commended her great faith and healed her.

Luke 8:42-48

Jesus healed a **nobleman's son.**

John 4:46-54

Jesus healed **a boy** who was suffering because of a demon.

Matthew 17:14-20

Jesus raised **a girl** from the dead.

Matthew 9:23-26

Jesus healed **a girl** who was troubled by a demon.

Matthew 15:21-28

THE OUTCASTS

 People in that day thought **WOMEN** were inferior to men (they could not have been more wrong!), but Jesus went out of His way to show how valuable women are. Women played important roles in Jesus's ministry.

 Most Jews would not eat with **GENTILES** (non-Jewish people) or go to their houses. But Jesus befriended Gentiles and loved them so much that He died on the cross to save them.

The name Magdalene designated the village she was from (Magdala, in the region of Galilee). It wasn't her last name.

A centurion was a Roman leader of 100 soldiers.

Jesus commended a **Canaanite woman** for her great faith and He healed her daughter.
Matthew 15:28

Jesus was obedient to **His mother** while growing up (Luke 2:51) and later, even from the cross, commissioned John to take care of her (John 19:25-27).

Early on, Jesus cast 7 demons out of **Mary Magdalene** (Luke 8:2). Later, she and other women witnessed His crucifixion (Matthew 27:55-56). Mary saw the empty tomb, and Jesus appeared to her first after His resurrection. He sent her to tell His disciples He had risen (John 20:1-18).

Jesus spoke to a **Samaritan woman** even though men did not usually talk to women they didn't know. The Samaritan woman spread the word about Jesus.
John 4:1-39

Jesus healed a **Roman centurion's** servant and commended the centurion's faith.
Matthew 8:5-13

How Jesus spent His final days on earth.

Palm SUNDAY
John 12:12-19

MONDAY
Mark 11:12-18

Busy TUESDAY
Matthew 21:23–25:46; Mark 11:20-25

WEDNESDAY
Luke 22:1-6

JESUS MAKES QUITE AN ENTRANCE ON A DONKEY

Did You Know:

Donkeys may not be as fast as horses, but they can pull twice their body weight. **x2**

Their large ears help them stay cool.

Donkeys can live more than 50 years.

If a donkey and zebra have a baby, it is called a zonkey.

People wave palm branches in praise.

Palm branches held special meaning for the Jewish people. They were used as part of the Feast of Tabernacles as a symbol for deliverance.

JESUS CURSES A FRUITLESS FIG TREE

The fig tree was a symbol of Israel.

The country's lack of spiritual fruit (like repentance) frustrated Jesus.

 =

fig tree with no fruit   **Jewish people** with no fruit

JESUS CLEANSES THE TEMPLE

The temple was intended to be a house of prayer and worship.

Money changers were taking advantage of all the Passover visitors. Even worse, they were set up in the court of the Gentiles, taking away the only area where the Gentiles could pray and worship God.

Temple Building

Court of the Gentiles

JESUS VISITS THE WITHERED FIG TREE

A fig tree is the third tree mentioned in the Bible.

1st Tree of life

2nd Tree of the knowledge of good and evil

3rd Adam and Eve used fig leaves to sew clothes for themselves.

JESUS TEACHES SOME PARABLES

Check out pages 38-39!

JESUS DEBATES AND DENOUNCES SCRIBES AND PHARISEES

Denounce (v.): a big word for publicly expressing disapproval

JESUS TEACHES ABOUT THE LAST DAYS

Check out pages 54-55!

CHIEF PRIESTS PLOT AGAINST JESUS

Did you know that politics existed even in Jesus's time?

The Jewish people wanted a king, but the Jewish leaders did not want that king to be Jesus. They killed Jesus to keep their political power.

JUDAS AGREES TO BETRAY JESUS FOR 30 PIECES OF SILVER

How much was 30 pieces of silver worth?

We don't know exactly what it would equal today, but we know that it was enough money to purchase a field.

Matthew 27:3-10

Nope, not Monday
Maundy (adj): comes from the Latin word for "command" and refers to the new commandment Jesus gave after washing the disciples' feet: "Love one another as I have loved you."

Why call this sad day "good"?
Ultimately, what happened was for our good, so we could be forgiven of our sins.

Maundy THURSDAY
Matthew 26:17-75; John 13–17

Good FRIDAY
Luke 23

Silent SATURDAY
Matthew 27:62-66

Easter SUNDAY
Matthew 28:1-15; Luke 24

JESUS WASHES THE DISCIPLES' FEET

Traditionally, considerate hosts had servants wash guests' stinky, smelly feet. Instead of a servant, Jesus washed the disciples' feet, showing how we are called to love each other.

JESUS AND THE DISCIPLES HAVE THE LAST SUPPER

The Last Supper is also known as...

Lord's Supper • Lord's Table • Holy Communion • Eucharist • breaking of bread • cup of blessing

Greek for Thanksgiving

JESUS PRAYS IN GETHSEMANE

JUDAS BETRAYS JESUS

Betrayed by a kiss. Ouch.

JESUS IS PUT ON TRIAL BY SANHEDRIN

Sanhedrin (n.): The highest court in Israel

PETER DENIES KNOWING JESUS

JESUS IS PUT ON TRIAL BY PONTIUS PILATE

Pilate was the Roman governor of Israel's region.

JESUS IS BEATEN AND CRUCIFIED

9:00 A.M.
Crucified with criminals
Soldiers gambled for His clothing
Cried out in thirst

12:00 P.M.
Darkness fell over the land
Cried out to God, "Why have you forsaken me?"
Prayed to God, "Into your hands I commit my spirit."

3:00 P.M.
Called out, "It is finished."
Bowed His head
Gave up His Spirit

Several miracles occurred at the time of Jesus's death.

The temple veil was torn.
The earth shook, and rocks split.
Graves were opened, and people were raised from the dead.

JESUS IS BURIED

The tomb was owned by a rich man, Joseph of Arimathea.

ROMAN SOLDIERS GUARD THE TOMB

Why guard a dead man?

Jesus predicted that He would raise from the dead. The religious leaders didn't want anyone to steal His body and pretend that He had done as He said.

Sealed the deal

In addition to guards and a stone blocking Jesus's tomb, a governmental seal (probably something like clay) was placed on the stone. This was likely imprinted with a Roman imperial symbol and attached to the stone with a rope. Anyone who could get past the guards would face an angry Roman government.

Matthew 27:66

Nope, not *that* kind of seal!

It was Sabbath

The Sabbath was a day of rest, and for the disciples, this one was also a day of waiting...

JESUS RISES FROM THE GRAVE ON THE THIRD DAY

But isn't this two days since His death?

"The third day" is a Jewish way of saying "the day after tomorrow."

JESUS APPEARS TO MARY MAGDALENE

JESUS APPEARS TO TWO PEOPLE ON THE ROAD TO EMMAUS

JESUS APPEARS TO TEN OF THE DISCIPLES

But weren't there 12 disciples?

Judas and Thomas were absent.
John 20:24

THE CRUCIFIXION

CRUCIFIXION (v.):
a way that the Romans killed criminals as punishment for their crime.

- thieves
- murderers
- insurrectionists
- rebels
- terrorists

INVENTED BY THE PERSIANS in 300–400 BC. The Roman Empire made it more common.

In Psalm 22:16-18, King David describes a harrowing execution. This prophesies how Jesus dies...but **1,000 years before He was born** and **centuries before Roman crucifixion was invented!**

KINDS OF CROSSES:

traditional cross shape   **T-shaped**   **X-shaped**

I-shaped   **upside-down cross**

Church tradition says the apostle Peter was crucified upside down, at his request, because he felt unworthy to die the same way as Jesus.

JESUS'S CRUCIFIXION

"My God, my God, why have you forsaken me?"
Matthew 27:46

Psalm 22:1

"Into your hands I commit my spirit."
Luke 23:46

Psalm 31:5

This was a common Jewish phrase recited before bedtime, **foreshadowing Jesus's crucifixion.**

"It is finished."
John 19:29-30

This phrase is the Greek word tetelestai, an accounting term meaning **"paid in full."**

His hands and feet were nailed to the cross, and then the cross was lifted upright.

People could take up to a few days to die on a cross.

It was Friday, and the Jews wanted to speed up Jesus's death because the Sabbath was the next day. **The Roman soldiers were going to break His legs to do this.**

OUCH!

Jesus died after about 6 hours on the cross, so the Roman soldiers never broke His legs. (John 19:33)

Psalm 22:14

Instead, they stuck a spear into His side to confirm He was dead. (John 19:34-37)

Zechariah 12:10

 = PROPHECY FULFILLED

THE RESURRECTION

WHEN JESUS DIED, EVERYONE WANTED TO CONFIRM WHAT HAPPENED.
JESUS HAD PREDICTED THAT HE WOULD RISE FROM THE DEAD,
THAT HE WAS THE MESSIAH.

WAS IT TRUE?

PROOF OF JESUS'S RESURRECTION

Was Jesus actually buried in the tomb?

 YES! He was **buried by Joseph of Arimathea and Nicodemus**—two influential and highly respected men who could testify to His burial. It would have been risky for these men to defend and protect Jesus (because of their social, religious, and political life).

Was Jesus's body in the tomb when it was was sealed?

 YES! The **low entrance** proves they had to be intentional to see that the body was there. (John 20:5)

 YES! The **Roman guards** would have ensured the body was in there before wasting their time guarding an empty tomb.

Could Jesus's body be confused with someone else's?

NO. The Bible says it was a *new tomb*. There were no other bodies inside—only Jesus's. His body couldn't be confused with anyone else's. (John 19:41)

Was the empty tomb a different tomb than He was buried in?

 NO. **The women knew** what tomb it was. They were there for the burial and returned to the same tomb on Easter Sunday.

NO. Those who investigated the empty tomb first, like Peter, **knew these were Jesus's burial cloths.** (John 20:5-7)

Was Jesus's body stolen from the tomb?

 NO. It was watched by Roman guards. The doorway/entrance was sealed and **could be opened only by Roman authorities**.

NO. When the burial cloths were found, they were **undisturbed** from how they were wrapped on Jesus's body. They would not have been touched by humans. (John 20:5-7)

Did Jesus escape?

 NO. The entrance was the **only way out** and watched by Roman guards. (Matthew 27:60)

 NO. The stone was so **large and heavy**, it would be impossible to move from the inside. The stone was placed in a groove that made it easy to roll into place but very difficult to remove.

What Do Jesus's CRUCIFIXION

He predicted His death and resurrection.
Matthew 16:21

This was God's plan from even before Jesus was born—to rescue the world!

He kept His promises.
Luke 24:6

Jesus confirmed that what He said about Himself IS TRUE— that He is the Messiah.

HIS DEATH WAS...

Get ready for some big words!

A Substitutionary Atonement

Atonement (n.): a covering for a wrongdoing; the price paid for a past sin.

 In the Old Testament, the Israelites sacrificed animals as a temporary payment (or covering) for their sins. They constantly had to make new sacrifices. But Jesus's sacrifice—as the Lamb of God—was perfect and permanent.

 **SIN =** ☠
Because we have sinned, we are all condemned to die.
Romans 5:12

Jesus took our sins from us and put them on Himself, like dirty clothes.
Isaiah 53:5-6

 **SIN ≠** ☠
So now, we do not need to die for our sin because Jesus already died for them!

A Ransom Paid for Our Sin

Ransom (n.): a payment to free someone from captivity.

Before we believe in Jesus, we are slaves to sin.
Romans 6:17-18

 PAID
Jesus paid a ransom to free us from sin.
1 Timothy 2:5-6

Because we are freed from our slavery to sin, we are now free to live for God!
Romans 8:1-4

A Propitiation

Propitiation (n.): the satisfaction of God's wrath.

Just like a good judge would not be good if she or he allowed a convicted criminal to avoid their punishment, God would not be good if He overlooked the sins humans commit.

God is a righteous Judge and must punish sin.

Jesus took the punishment we deserved for our sin.
1 Peter 2:24

Because Jesus took our punishment, God is no longer angry at us about our sin.
Romans 5:9

Our Reconciliation to God

Reconciliation (n.): the restoration of a broken relationship.

While we were sinners, we were God's enemies, rebelling against Him as King.

Jesus made peace between us and the Father.
Romans 5:10-11

Now that Jesus has taken away God's anger, we can be friends with God.

An Example to Us

When Jesus died on the cross, He gave us an example of how to trust God when we suffer and endure persecution. 1 Peter 2:21-23

FOLLOW ME

and **RESURRECTION** Mean for Us?

He defeated death once and for all.
2 Timothy 1:10

Jesus's resurrection proved His divinity.

He defeated Satan, and He holds the keys of death and Hades.
Revelation 1:18

This was God's ultimate plan to defeat the enemy.

Throughout the Bible, we were promised Jesus would defeat Satan...and Satan would be punished.

From the beginning (Genesis 3:14-15) and throughout the Bible, **Jesus's resurrection is a promise of victory** (Romans 16:20).

As the perfect exalted Judge, Jesus will deliver Satan's punishment with

Eternal fire · Matthew 25:41
Condemnation · John 16:11
Torment in a lake of burning sulfur · Revelation 20:10

JESUS GUARANTEED OUR FUTURE RESURRECTION
God is not the God of the dead but of the living! Matthew 22:32

Through Jesus, we will also be resurrected...
John 14:19

...when Jesus returns to Earth.
1 Thessalonians 4:16-17

We will have resurrection bodies...
1 Corinthians 15:35-50

...that won't die!
1 Corinthians 15:50-54

...won't feel pain!
Revelation 21:4

...will be physical, real, and recognizable!
Luke 24:36-43

And they'll be like Jesus's resurrected body...
1 Corinthians 15:49

...so that we, too, can experience complete justice, peace, joy, and satisfaction in heaven.
Luke 22:29-30

JESUS, THE...

 **PRIEST**

 PROPHET

 KING

In the Old Testament (OT) God used special types of leaders to interact with His people: **priests**, **prophets**, and **kings**. Jesus—as the One chosen to save the world—was all three.

Feeling fancy? Call these the "offices" of Christ and really impress your friends.

PRIEST: A priest acts as a go-between, representing the people to God.

THE ROLE OF AN **OT** PRIEST

They presented animal sacrifices and met with God in the innermost part of the temple.

FAMOUS **OT** PRIESTS

Aaron   **Samuel**   **Ezra**

Animal sacrifice is weird. So why did they do it?

Quick answer—God told them to offer animal sacrifice for the forgiveness of sin (Leviticus 4). So why don't we do this today?

Because of JESUS! Let's look closer...

	OT PRIESTS		**JESUS**
Who needed the sacrifice? Hebrews 7:27		Priests and the people	Only the people because Jesus had no sin
When did the sacrifice happen? Hebrews 9:25-26		Each year on the Day of Atonement	Once and for all on the cross
What was sacrificed? Hebrews 9:12		The blood of bulls and goats	Jesus's own blood
How effective was the sacrifice? Hebrews 10:4,10		The blood of bulls and goats cannot take away sin	The blood of Jesus takes away our sin forever

 **MEANING FOR US...**

Jesus understands our weaknesses, our temptations, and our suffering because He too was human.
But He was without sin, which makes His sacrifice for us on the cross perfect to cover all our sins.
Jesus is clearly the priest we need to represent us to God. (Hebrews 4:14-16)

PROPHET: A prophet speaks to the people for God and represents God to the people.

THE ROLE OF AN **OT** PROPHET

God used the prophets to declare His commands, warn people of sin, and give them direction.

FAMOUS **OT** PROPHETS

Moses   Elijah   Isaiah   Jeremiah

JESUS as the *ULIMATE PROPHET*

Moses predicts God will send the ultimate prophet.
Deuteronomy 18:15

Peter declares that Jesus is the one who fulfilled Moses's prophecy.
Acts 3:23-26

 He's God's Son, so He speaks for God with all authority.
Hebrews 1:1-2

Like prophets, He spoke the Word of God. But unlike other prophets, He IS the Word.
John 1:14

MEANING FOR US...

Have you ever wondered what God might do or say about something? You can know the answer! **Look to Jesus, the ultimate prophet.** More than any other person, Jesus knows God. Through His words and actions we can know the heart and mind of God.

KING: A king rules over God's people.

THE ROLE OF AN **OT** KING

Was suppose to be a fair ruler that applied God's law. But too often they used their role to get rich and powerful.

FAMOUS **OT** KINGS

David   Solomon   Josiah

I'm only 8 years old!

A descendent of David will reign forever. 2 Samuel 7:16

JRIGINAL PLAN
GOD IS KING!
1 Samuel 8:7

BUT...

NEW PLAN
...people be crazy. They need a ~~HUMAN RULER~~ **HUMAN KING**
Judges 21:25

Let's see if I measure up.

AND THEN...

EVEN NEWER, BETTER PLAN
God is back as King through Jesus.
Matthew 22:42-44

Jesus is crowned as King after He ascends into heaven.
Acts 2:32-35

This plan rules!

MEANING FOR US...

If Jesus is our King, then we should obey Him. We know He will rule over us with justice and fairness.

THE RETURN

THE FIRST COMING
DOWN TO EARTH
Galatians 4:4-5

ASCENSION
BACK TO HEAVEN
Acts 1:4-11

THE INCARNATION

God taking on humanity as a man.

The **Word** was made flesh, and dwelt among us.
John 1:14 KJV

Jesus

THE ASCENSION

After His resurrection, Jesus ascended to heaven, hidden by a cloud.

ascend (v.): rise

His coming was humble, ordinary.

| Born as a baby in a manger. | Lived in Nazareth, a poor and undesirable area of Israel. | Earthly father, Joseph, was a carpenter. |

WHERE IS JESUS NOW?

He is at the right hand of the Father.
Colossians 3:1

THE TRIUMPHAL ENTRY

Hosanna... Son of David!

WHAT IS JESUS DOING NOW?

Jesus rides into Jerusalem as King on a donkey.
Prophesied in Zechariah 9:9

 Donkeys were symbols of peace.

Crowds praise Him as King, waving palm branches.

 The palms symbolized the Jewish nation and victory over their enemies.

The crowds placed their cloaks on the ground for the donkey to walk on. That was a symbol of submission to a king.

He speaks on our behalf as our high priest.
Hebrews 9:24

He rules as the head of the church.
Ephesians 1:22-23

He holds His creation together.
Colossians 1:15-17

THE SECOND COMING
DOWN TO EARTH, PART DEUX
Revelation 19:11-16

Wearing "many crowns"

Symbolizes He is the King of kings

With "a sharp sword" coming from His mouth

Symbolizes the Word of God

The record for largest sword ever swallowed is 28 inches! Don't try this at home, kids!!!

Riding a white horse

Symbolizes Jesus returning in victory

With "a name written on him that no one knows but he himself"

King of Kings
Lord of Lords

That's what you call a glow up!

"Called Faithful and True"

Eyes "like blazing fire"

Wearing "a robe dipped in blood"

Symbolizing His judgment of those who refuse to honor Him as King.

Named the "Word of God"

Symbolizes that He is the one who reveals God to us.

With the name "KING OF KINGS AND LORD OF LORDS"—"on his robe and on his thigh"

WHAT WILL JESUS BE DOING FOR ETERNITY?

He will dwell with His people and rule over them as the one true King.
Revelation 21:3

He will be the New Jerusalem's lamp/light.
Revelation 22:5

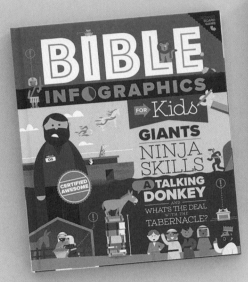
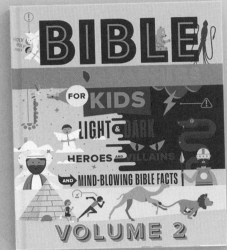
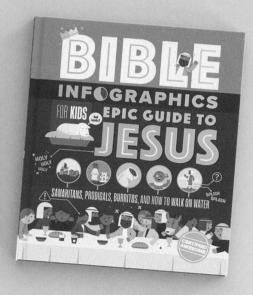

Time to meet the family!

I guess things are moving fast, huh?

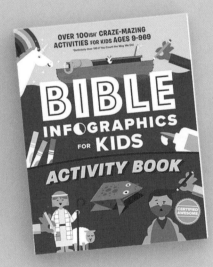

And would you look at that? Even the littlest one won't be lost in the shuffle!

Hi! We're here for the free stuff.

Learn more or download free stuff* at
BibleInfographics.com

*Flash cards, trading cards, activities, game rules, and other wacky things we haven't thought of yet.